COLL

island of the Hebrides

Diana Ogg

Head of Humanities,
Sholing Girls' School, Southampton

Dryad Press Limited   London

The Islands series

What have these people in common: Enid Blyton, Daniel Defoe, Robert Louis Stevenson and Roy Plomley? They have all written about islands, islands as places of adventure or fantasy. Think for a moment of the many stories or events that are associated with islands. What do you know about "Fortress Falklands", or Alcatraz, or the adventures of Robinson Crusoe? Islands have long held a special appeal and this series sets out to explore the fascination of islands.

Every island is unique, with a different location, a distinctive history and a particular personality. And yet about them all there are similarities, too. Island cultures are distinct because they are isolated, set apart from mainstream societies. They can be remote, places of refuge or sanctuary, where you can "get away from it all"! Monks and rich recluses have chosen island homes because they wanted seclusion. Other island inhabitants have had no choice in the matter because the isolation of islands also makes them ideal places for imprisonment or exile; Alcatraz and Elba certainly have that one thing in common.

In many cases, too, the remoteness of islands has meant that life for people, animals and plants has remained undisturbed by the progress and change of the mainlands. Forms and ways of life survive which elsewhere have become extinct, as is the case on the remote and beautiful islands of the Galapagos.

Another common feature of island life is that it can present similar problems of survival. Is there enough land to grow food and to keep animals? Is there an ample supply of water?

Why do islands become deserted?

Islands, therefore, can be places of challenge where you must learn to survive, fending for yourself on limited resources, or places of isolation and retreat where you dream about the good life – and listen to your desert island discs!

In each book of the series the author's purpose is to explore the uniqueness of a particular island and to convey the special appeal of the island. There is no common approach but in every case the island can be seen as a system in which a society is linked to its physical environment. An island culture can show clearly how the natural environment influences the ways people make a living. It also shows how people learn to modify or change that environment to make life better or more secure. This is very much a geographical view of islands, but the ideas and study skills used in the books are not limited to those of the geographer. The one controlling idea of the series is that islands are special places; small enough to know well and varied enough to illustrate the rich diversity of environments and lifestyles from all parts of the world. Islands can be places of social experiment or strategic importance, of simple survival or extravagance. Islands are the world in miniature.

John Bentley
Series editor

For details of other books in the Islands series please write to Dryad Press Limited, 8 Cavendish Square, London W1M 0AJ.

Contents

ACKNOWLEDGMENTS

This book is dedicated to my parents for introducing me to Coll.

Special thanks go to the people of Coll who have helped me in so many different ways and without whom this book would not have been possible.

My thanks are due to many people for their help: to John Bentley and Ruth Taylor for their patience, to Claire Cook for her typing and to Sue Stokes for her suggestions. Many thanks to Peter Mcdonnell for his endless encouragement.

All illustrations are by the author, with the exception of the frontispiece and figures 10, 30, 40, 42, 43, courtesy of Jane Austin; figures 19, 20, 24, courtesy of Kevin and Julie Oliphant; figures 25, 28, 53, courtesy of Andy Parfitt; figures 27, 38, 49, 51, courtesy of John Ogg; figure 33, courtesy of Peter Mcdonnell; figure 45, courtesy of Hebridean Herbals; figures 46, 47, 48, courtesy of Project Trust; figure 8, courtesy of the Argyll and Bute District Council; figure 50 (Crown copyright), courtesy of the Controller of Her Majesty's Stationery Office. Figures 2, 3, 9, 11, 23, 36, 44 and on page 63, were drawn by R.F. Brien.

Cover photographs
The photographs on the front cover show a view from Ben Hogh, a wild orchid (courtesy of Andy Parfitt), the Project Trust Selection Centre, and sheep on the pier at Arinagour. The photographs on the back cover show Calum the Post and Struan.

© Diana Ogg 1988
First published 1988

Typeset by Tek-Art Ltd, Kent
and printed and bound in Great Britain by
Richard Clay Ltd,
Chichester, Sussex
for the publishers Dryad Press Limited,
8 Cavendish Square, London W1M 0AJ

ISBN 0 8521 9728 4

1

This is Coll

Miles of golden sands, deep-blue sea and brilliant sunshine. Where are the people? Do you find Crossapol beach attractive? What do you think could be some of the disadvantages of a holiday here?

"Attention please. We are now approaching the Island of Coll. Will car drivers please stand by their vehicles? We hope you have enjoyed your journey. Thank you for travelling with Caledonian Macbrayne."

1 *Crossapol beach on the island of Coll.*

This announcement over the ship's loudspeakers sends a few people down to the car deck. It is packed full with 40 cars, but only 7 of them are going to Coll. The rest are heading for Tiree.

2 *Scotland and the location of Coll.*

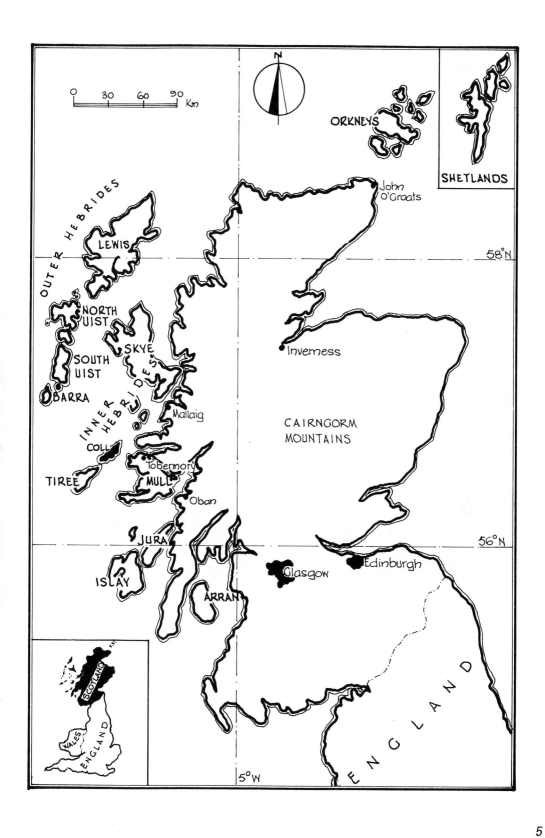

O 30 60 90 Km

N

ORKNEYS

SHETLANDS

John O'Groats

58°N

OUTER HEBRIDES

LEWIS

NORTH UIST

SKYE

SOUTH UIST

BARRA

INNER HEBRIDES

Mallaig

COLL

TIREE

Tobermory

MULL

Oban

JURA

ISLAY

ARRAN

Inverness

CAIRNGORM MOUNTAINS

56°N

Glasgow

Edinburgh

ENGLAND

SCOTLAND

WALES

ENGLAND

5°W

ENGLAND

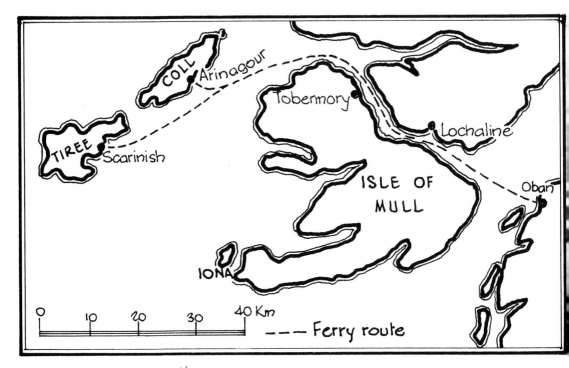

Coll is an island in the Inner Hebrides, a group of islands off the west coast of Scotland. Occasionally in the summer it might look like a tropical island, as in the photograph, but as we shall discover, the island is often very different in a number of ways.

Which of the Hebridean islands shown on fig. 2 is the biggest? Which is the smallest? How far is Coll from the most northern Hebridean island? How far is it from your home to Coll? Would you expect to find any differences between the climate of your home area and the climate of Coll? If so, what would these be?

The boat had left Oban in a heavy mist and passengers saw little of the scenery until Tobermory, where the sun had greeted them and they had enjoyed the sight of the brightly painted houses along the waterfront, with many colourful yachts in the busy harbour. Most people spent the last hour of the journey sitting on the boat's decks, viewing the islands across the shimmering sea.

Use the map and timetable to find out which islands the ship calls at. Which other islands do

3   The ship's route.

you think passengers will be able to see during their journey? What time does the boat arrive at Coll during the summer months?

Two teenage girls heading for a holiday on Tiree viewed the village of Arinagour at the head of Loch Eatharna Bay, from the boat's deck.

"Is that the only village on Coll? There are very few houses there. Are there more than that on Tiree?" asked one, sounding rather worried.

COLL and TIREE	OBAN-COLL-TIREE			
	Until 28 September			From
	Fri	Sat	Mon & Wed	Tues, Th
OBAN .... dep.	0530	0600	0815	07
LOCHALINE ● .... dep.	—	—	0920	—
TOBERMORY ..... dep.	—	0800	1030	08
COLL .... arr.	1115A	0945	1215	10
TIREE .... arr.	0930	1045	1315	11

"Aye, that's the only village, but Coll's not that bad," replied her friend. "We've had some really good holidays there. Tiree is only a little bigger, but it's got loads more people on it. It's amazing really how two places so close to each other can be so different."

Boat time

"Boat time" on Coll is very important, providing the island's only regular link with the mainland. In the summer months the village bustles for an hour or more after the boat arrives. People

5 Arinagour village, close to the shores of Loch Eatharna Bay. Notice how much space there is between the buildings. Can you see any trees?

are fetching supplies – the locals refer to their shopping as their "messages". They enjoy a chat with friends in the village High Street. Many others are there just for the excitement of seeing the boat come in.

John James, the island's pier-master, shares a joke with the crew as they unload the visiting cars and freight for the island. There are lots of different things being delivered to Coll. One trailer contains a mixed load of loaves of bread,

4 Timetable of the ship's sailings.

We regret that only passengers holding sleeping berth reservations are allowed on board vessels overnight. **Table 15**

e and Tobermory) i 🚗 Ⓡ ✗ 🍷 🛏		Until 28 September			From 1 October
		Fri	Sat	Mon & Wed	Tues, Thurs & Sat
.... dep.		1015	1145	1400	1215
.... dep.		1130	1300	1520	1330
)RY .... arr.			1430	1650	1450
IE ● ...... arr.		—	—	1750	—
.... arr.		1500	1630	1900	1645
)n.St. 🚆 arr.		2102	2102	—	2102
) 🚌 . arr.		2050	2050	—	2050

CODE:

A — Sails via Tiree.

● — Calls to set down and uplift passengers only.

🛏 — Are available at Oban on Sunday, Tuesday, Thursday and Friday nights until 27 September. Monday, Wednesday, Friday nights from 30 September must be claimed between 2100 and 2300 hours (except) Friday nights until 27 September when they must be claimed between 2200 and 2300 hours. Cars for early morning sailing will be loaded previous night, provided they are available on the pier, on arrival of the last sailing of the day.

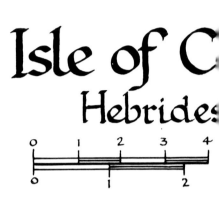

posts have also arrived for him, so he will have to make two journeys between the pier and his farm at Cliad. Use the map of Coll to find out how far John has to travel from Cliad to the "new pier".

Isle of C
Hebrides

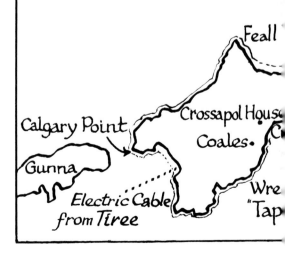

6   The Columba *at the Coll pier.*

cans of concentrated liquids for dipping sheep, and sheets of asbestos roofing. Another trailer is filled with boxes of tinned food and bottles of lemonade. John English drives up and down the pier on a small tractor, towing the trailers to the pier store. He has to drive carefully, as the pier is very crowded with people meeting the boat.

Allan Brodie is meeting two cows. They're delighted to be out of the small pen they shared on the boat and leap about as they are driven into Allan's trailer.

Alec Arileod (his name is actually MacLennan, but he's lived in Arileod for many years) is there to meet the freezer he ordered from the mainland six weeks ago.

John Galbraith has come with his tractor to collect ten tonnes of cattle feed. Some fencing

Kevin Oliphant is collecting beer, wines and spirits for the hotel. He is very glad to see that the whole order has arrived on time, as supplies have been running very low.

Janet Stewart meets a family arriving for a week's holiday.

7   A postcard map.

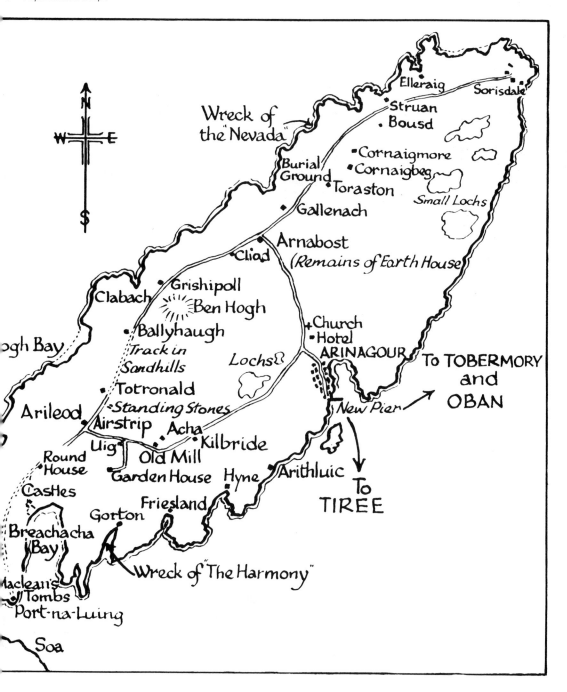

Calum the Post is there to collect the island's mail. If he can sort it quickly, then he can go around the island delivering post and collecting mail for the boat returning from Tiree. Use the timetable, fig. 4, to find out how long Calum will have on a Monday before he has to be back on the pier to send the island's mail away to Oban.

Robert Sturgeon is fetching people who have come to stay at the guest house. Two of them are wearing binoculars and carrying cameras. They have come to Coll especially to watch the birds, seals and otters.

Kenneth Stewart is meeting a new Simmental bull. It takes some coaxing to get the roaring animal to walk off the car deck, and people move cautiously to one side as it is driven slowly up the pier.

The boat calls at Coll four times a week in the summer and three times a week in the winter. You can see from the timetable that it does not always arrive at the same time. On which day would you choose to travel if you wanted the shortest possible time on the boat? How much longer would you have to add to your journey to reach Oban from your home?

Arinagour

The village of Arinagour takes up only a very small part of the island, but it is very important to the 140 Collachs (people of Coll) and to visitors. It is the only centre for shopping, with its two small shops and a post office, and for social activities, which take place at the village hall. It also has the island's only hotel, with its bars and games room. Arinagour is the only place on Coll where you can buy fuel. The village also contains the island's two churches. See how many of these places you can find on the plan of Arinagour (fig. 8).

Not everybody on Coll lives in the village. Some people live in very isolated houses that are difficult to reach. Not all the houses on Coll are lived in for the whole year. Some of them are holiday houses. Use the map, fig. 9, to help

8   Local plan of Arinagour. How far would you have to walk from the pier to the Post Office (PO)?

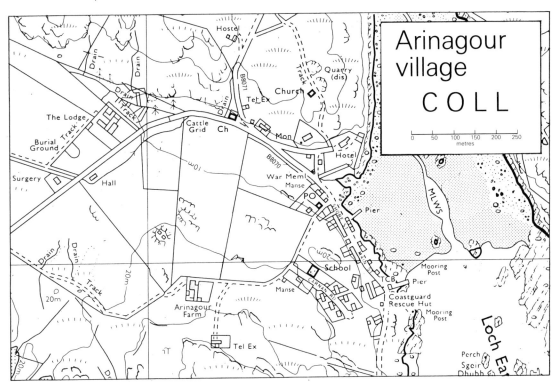

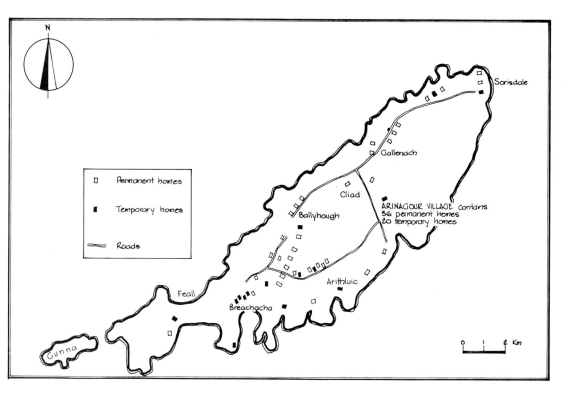

Legend:
- □ Permanent homes
- ■ Temporary homes
- ═ Roads

ARINAGOUR VILLAGE contains
36 permanent homes
20 temporary homes

(Labels on map: Sorisdale, Gallenach, Cliad, Ballyhaugh, Arithluic, Feall, Breachacha, Gunna)

Scale: 0 1 2 Km

you work out how many houses are permanent dwellings and how many are used just for holidays. Which houses are furthest from the village and which do you think will be the easiest to reach, or the most "accessible"?

Visitors to Coll on a beautiful summer's day see the island at its best, but the weather can change very quickly. Weeks can pass without passengers getting a glimpse of the island, as violent storms blow across the Atlantic.

The Collachs have had to learn to live with the variety of weather. They have learnt to cope

9 *Permanent and temporary homes on Coll.*

with problems such as shortage of supplies, that can be the result of long periods when boats cannot reach Coll. The island's isolation is seen as a problem by some, but as an advantage by others. To a great extent, the Collachs' way of life is a reflection of the environment in which they live.

Throughout this book we shall be looking at some of the different aspects of Coll that make it a unique island.

2

Yesterday to today

People have been living on Coll for hundreds of years. In that time many different things have happened to the island. If we are to become familiar with the Coll of today, then it is important that we understand some of the major events that have taken place in the island's history.

Look carefully at some of the important dates in Coll's history. Use an atlas to discover how far the Norsemen travelled from Norway to Coll in the year 1000.

Important dates in Coll's history

8th century A.D.	Viking invasions of the Hebrides, including Coll. (Vikings were pirates from Scandinavia.)
1000 approximately	Coll is an important Norse settlement (i.e. a settlement for people from Norway).
Late 13th century	Coll belongs to the Macdougall family from Lorne (an area of Argyllshire near Oban). Robert Bruce fights many battles to win land and keep Scotland independent from England. He gives Coll to Macdonald of Islay.
15th century	Coll given to John Maclean, founder of the Maclean of Coll family. Breachacha Castle built (fig. 10).
1750	New castle built close to the original one. Population reaches 1500.
1841	Potato famine.
1846	Coll sold to John Stewart.
1856	Population approximately 140.
1980	

10 Breachacha Castle. Notice how close to the sea the castle is built.

A major landowner in Scotland is known as a "Laird". Today, although he no longer owns the whole island, Kenneth Stewart, a descendant of John Stewart, has the title of "Laird of Coll".

When John Stewart bought the island in 1856, many changes occurred. He was a very knowledgeable farmer and reorganized the island's farming, replacing most of the many small crofting units with a few large dairy units.

Crofting used to be a very important way of life in many areas of Scotland. A "crofter" rented his croft, generally no more than four hectares in size, from the Laird. (A football pitch is one hectare in size.) The crofter produced food for his own family from the land, and often worked for the Laird as well.

John Stewart increased the rents of the Coll crofters so much that many could not afford to pay. The potato famine which had begun in 1846 made their situation more desperate. Hundreds of Collachs were forced to emigrate.

What is the difference in population between 1841 and 1980?

Many Collachs emigrated to live in towns on the mainland of Scotland. Others went to Canada and to Australia. Look at an atlas map of the world. How far is it from Coll to (a) Perth in Australia and (b) Newfoundland in Canada? During the nineteenth century such journeys might have taken many weeks. Not everybody survived. Those who did would have found it very difficult to return to Coll.

Today, descendants of those who had to leave Coll visit the island for holidays. What do you think it is that makes them travel so far to visit the homes of their ancestors?

The people

There are about 140 people living on Coll today. Fig. 11 shows how the workforce are employed on Coll and in Britain as a whole. Which type of employment is (a) the most important and (b) the least important on the island?

Coll can be called a "farming community", since so many of the island's workers (about

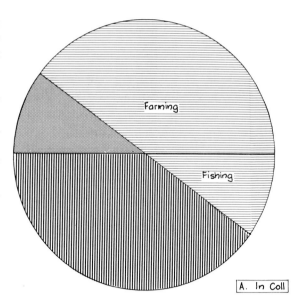

A. In Coll

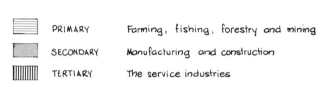

PRIMARY   Farming, fishing, forestry and mining

SECONDARY   Manufacturing and construction

TERTIARY   The service industries

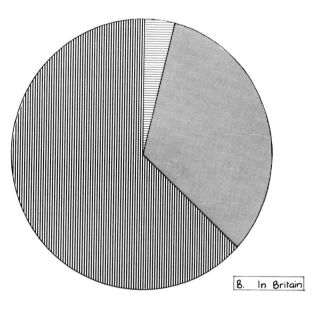

B. In Britain

11   Types of employment.

13

40%) are employed in farming. Fishing employs 10%.

In Britain as a whole, only a very small percentage (less than 4%) of the workforce are employed in primary industries. There used to be a much higher percentage working on the land. Can you think why the number has decreased in Britain and why so many remain farming on Coll?

About one-third of Britain's workers are employed in secondary industries. This section, too, used to employ a higher percentage. What do you think has taken over the jobs?

Well over 60% are employed in the service or tertiary industries in Britain. This figure has increased enormously this century. What sort of jobs does this category include?

Service workers on Coll

SERVICE	PEOPLE EMPLOYED	COMMENT
SCHOOL	1 teacher 1 part-time cook 1 part-time cleaner 2 part-time drivers	Takes pupils aged 5-11 years only.
SHOPS	2 full-time	See chapter 5 "Shops and shopping" page 23.
ROADS	2 full-time	All roads are single-track and unfenced. Animals wander across roads. There is no garage on Coll, so cars do not require an MOT.
REFUSE COLLECTION	1 part-time	Collection by tractor and dust cart every Saturday. Bins must be carried to the nearest part of the road for collection.
LIBRARY	Nobody is employed. Borrowers help themselves to books.	Open school hours. Books change 2 or 3 times a term. Self-service. Books sent over from mainland.
EMERGENCY SERVICES		See chapter 10, "999 emergency", page 52.
CALEDONIAN MACBRAYNE	2 part-time	3 ferries a week in winter, 4 in summer.
POST OFFICE	1 full-time post mistress 1 part-time post master (Calum the Post)	Postal collections and deliveries on ferry days only.
ELECTRICITY	1 part-time	Men sent over from the mainland for major works.
TELEPHONE	1 part-time	
HOTEL	2 full-time	See chapter 6, "Summer visitors", page 27.
GUEST HOUSE		
SELF-CATERING ACCOMMODATION		

12 Calum the Post in Arinagour. Notice the bare rock showing in the land behind him, and in picture 13.

13 One of the island's four post-boxes.

How much bigger is the percentage of people employed in primary industries on Coll than in Britain generally?

Which of the services in the table do you think would create "seasonal employment", or employ extra people during the summer months?

Several people are employed in more than one job. John James, for example, has the following part-time jobs: pier-master, lobster fisherman, airstrip master, hydroelectric worker, school driver. He is also chief coastguard and serves in the island's Fire Brigade. Why do you think it is necessary for people to have several part-time jobs on Coll, instead of one full-time?

How many people do you know who have jobs like John James?

Think about the jobs done by your friends' parents. Describe and try to explain the differences in employment between your local area and Coll.

3

Collachs and ceilidhs

Show day

"Take your partners for a strip the willow," announces Neil Galbraith, Master of Ceremonies at the Coll Show Dance. People immediately move into the centre of the village hall, ready to do this ever popular, very energetic, traditional dance.

The annual Horticultural Show on the first Friday of August is always a big event on the island, and most people have the day off work to join in the fun. Islanders and visitors prepare entries for the competition classes which include baking, knitting, vegetables, eggs and sheep. Judging takes place in the morning. In the afternoon there are children's sports events, a Scottish dancing display, a cross country run, a tug-of-war between islanders and visitors, and several other entertainments. A bar behind the hall keeps everything running with a merry swing!

Are there any events similar to the Coll Show held in your neighbourhood?

At about 10 o'clock in the evening of the

14 Scottish dancing display at the Coll Show. Find the hall on the local plan of Arinagour (fig. 8).

show day, a band, usually a man with an accordion, sometimes accompanied by a guitarist or a drummer, gets ready for the dance. This, and the show prize-giving dance on the following Friday, are always very well supported and might continue until 2 or 3 in the morning. There is no disco dancing, but young and old, locals and visitors alike join in with traditional dances like the Highland Scottish, the Gay Gordons, Eightsome Reels and the Bonnie Dundee. Even absolute beginners tend to love the dancing. It doesn't matter if they cannot get it right. Everyone is there to have fun and they certainly make sure that they do!

During the summer months there might be as many as five Friday evening dances, but in the winter they are rare. Can you think why?

Leisure time

There are no cinemas, discos, ice-rinks, swimming pools or other leisure facilities on Coll. Islanders have to arrange their own social events. The table shows you some of the activities that are arranged on the island.

15 Enjoying a drink from the bar at the Show.

Regular social activities on Coll

Weekly:	Playing pool and darts at the Hotel.
	Womens' keep fit.
	"Knitting Bee" in the winter.
Monthly:	Women's Guild.
Occasional dances	

Think about your own life. How many things that you enjoy doing now would you miss if you lived on Coll? Is there any Coll activity that you think you would enjoy in the winter months? Make a diary of social events in your neighbourhood and compare it with what is available on Coll.

Many Collachs have not been islanders all their lives but have moved to Coll for a variety of reasons. The following comments indicate some of their thoughts about life on Coll compared to the mainland.

"It was very difficult when I first moved here, like coming to another world. Now I wouldn't change it. There is absolutely nothing I really miss."

"I miss clothes shops occasionally. It's O.K. buying from a catalogue, but I do enjoy being

able to see and compare clothes in the shops."

"I enjoy living here but I miss my family a lot. I also miss swimming pools, hairdressers, going out for meals, and take-aways."

"I miss friends, sports centres and pub crawls."

"Coll is a great place to bring up children. There's no traffic to worry about. They can play in the fields and on the beaches. It is a very healthy life and children very often see both their parents during the day. There is very little child-adult segregation, so children grow up used to mixing with adults."

"I miss papers being delivered on time."

"Sometimes I miss dressing up to go somewhere really smart, but most of the time I love living in wellies."

What do you think you would miss most if you went to live on Coll?

16   *Enjoying a story at a ceilidh.*

Ceilidhs

Traditionally, a ceilidh (pronounced "caylee") means an informal gathering of people for singing and story-telling. Collachs enjoy a good ceilidh and, particularly during the summer months, many households ceilidh into the early hours of the morning.

New Year

New Year, or "Hogmanay" as it is called in Scotland, is an important occasion. Collachs might spend several days visiting each other's homes for ceilidhs and to wish everyone a Happy New Year. Whisky is the traditional drink and those celebrating Hogmanay toast the New Year with a drink from everyone they meet. The festivities can get very merry!

Are there any traditional festivities for New Year where you live?

4

One teacher, one school

Think about the primary school you went to. How many pupils were there in your class? How many teachers were there in the school? It is quite likely that several of your friends from that school are now in the same form as you in secondary school.

There is only one primary school on Coll, in the village of Arinagour. All children from the ages of 5 to 11 years attend this school. The number of pupils seldom exceeds 10 and is often nearer to 5.

Mainland primary schools are generally situated in areas where many children live. On Coll, the children might live several miles from school. There is no bus service, but two people are employed as part-time drivers to do the "school run". They collect the children for morning school and return them home at the end of the afternoon. Children meet the car at the nearest part of the road to their homes.

How far would children living at Crossapol House have to travel to meet the car? (See fig. 7.)

Even if there is only one child attending, the

17 Arinagour school.

teacher must keep the school open. The daily routine is similar to that of any other primary school in Britain, with a 20-minute break in the morning and an hour for lunch. All the children stay for a school lunch, which is freshly cooked each day. They can play in the school grounds which are often grazed by sheep.

Why is it impossible for the children to organize a lunchtime game of football?

The pupils certainly have the benefit of a lot of individual attention from the teacher, but they lack the stimulation of other pupils of their own age.

Think about your primary school life. Which lessons would have been different if you had been one of only five in the class? Do you think you would have enjoyed them any more or any less?

Away to High School

In their last year at the Coll school, the pupils visit the High School in Oban where most will go, as boarders, for their secondary education. A school of 1300 pupils often comes as quite a shock after the few in Arinagour school. Occasionally, a Coll child might be sent to the much smaller secondary school on Tiree, but there is no accommodation available and so he or she has to lodge with a family.

Asked what he would miss about Coll, an eleven-year-old boy, about to start in Oban, replied: "Coll bogs, the beaches and the dogs at home," but he was looking forward to "a swimming pool, cinema, space invaders, ice cream vans and shops". Asked what made Oban different from Coll, the same boy replied: "Oban has got police, shops, more people, a

job centre, more cars and trains and lots of 'phones. Oban has hospitals, fire engines, punks and skinheads."

Parents often find it very difficult when their eleven-year-olds leave home. The children from many islands live in school hostels in Oban, but, weather permitting, will see their parents for a few days once every four or six weeks.

The following comments from Coll children at school in Oban will give you some idea of their lifestyles:

Alec, an eleven-year-old boy, just a few weeks after arriving in Oban: "The first couple of weeks I was really nervous. . . . I miss my brother the most, then I miss fishing and the actual island, and my parents."

A first-year girl, Fiona, loved the school but hated living in the hostel: "At night the girls often get really homesick. It can be very sad."

A fifteen-year-old girl, Morag, speaks very fondly about her life at Coll primary school: "The most important thing about it was that we could go home every night to our own houses and our own beds. Our parents were always around when we needed them." She goes on

18 *The freedom of Coll. How do you think this shows the "freedom" that Morag speaks of? In the foreground you can see the coarse machair grass of the sand dunes behind Crossapol Bay. The hollows that you can see are the remains of older sand dunes. They contain many types of grasses that sheep can graze. The land is not fertile enough for growing crops.*

to talk about Oban: "It was hard at first, but after the first year it didn't seem too bad. I often miss my family, but most of all I miss the freedom and friendliness of Coll. . . . I miss the animals too. There aren't any sheep or cows in Oban!" She concludes: "People don't realize that it is two totally different lifestyles and while you're in one place you have to put the other completely out of your mind."

A fifth-year boy, Duncan, talks about Oban: "When I first started I found having to do my own washing, ironing and mending was a real pain. I used to really enjoy having it done for me whenever I went home. I really enjoy the variety of activities available in and out of school in Oban, though I miss shooting and fishing on Coll."

"Did you find it difficult when you started at Oban?"

"Not really. There were so many new things to do. I loved being able to play football and do field sports, though it took me a while to catch up with children from the mainland who had been doing these sports for years."

Asked "Do you enjoy living in the hostel?", Duncan replied, "Aye, it's all right. There's a games room we can use in our spare time. Boys share bedrooms for three. All the lower school pupils share a study, but in the upper school we have the benefit of a study bedroom between three . . . that's much better."

"Will you live on Coll when you leave school?"

"Doubt it. There's no work."

"If there was, would you?"

"Possibly."

Duncan enjoys going home for a few days at a time, but finds that the seven-week summer holiday is really too long a time away from the friends he has made in Oban. He misses the social activities and would really prefer to go back to Coll for several odd weeks spread through the year, than for one long stretch.

Think carefully about the comments above. Imagine your family lives on Coll. What do you think you would find most difficult about going to school in Oban? What do you think you would enjoy?

What does Morag's comment about the "freedom and friendliness of Coll" tell us about the island? Do you feel this way about the area in which you live?

5

Shops and shopping

How often do you go into town to go shopping? Perhaps once or twice a week? You might not actually buy anything, but the chances are that you often spend some time just wandering around the shops looking at things you might like to buy.

Coll has two shops and both are privately owned. The "Hotel Shop" belongs to the Oliphants, who also own the Coll Hotel. The two shops sell a variety of convenience goods such as groceries and household requirements. The Hotel Shop also sells petrol and Calor gas and the other sells newspapers.

19 The Hotel Shop. A modern building made with wood and bricks imported from the mainland.

20 The Hotel Shop has an off-licence.

The shops are open every day except Sundays in the summer, but in the winter they open only on "boat days". How often is that? Can you think why half the newspapers in the winter are out of date when they are sold in Arinagour?

Getting supplies

All the supplies for the shops have to come by ferry, and the shop owners must pay the cost of transporting the goods (freight) by boat. This can be expensive, especially if any of the goods are bulky.

All frozen food has to be very well wrapped to survive the journey to Coll, as there is no cold storage on the boat. One summer's day a trailer full of goods for the Coll shops was loaded on to the boat in Oban. On the top of the goods was placed a parcel of frozen meat. That day a storm blew and the boat didn't call at Coll for two days. By then the meat had thawed and blood was everywhere. Much of the trailer-load of goods had to be destroyed. The shopkeeper still had to pay freight for the trailer of goods, even though most of it was unfit to sell by the time it reached Coll.

Look at the table of the cost of goods on Coll. It shows the results of a survey in July 1985, comparing the cost of shopping for 18 convenience goods in Coll and in a supermarket on the mainland. The figures indicate the percentage difference in price.

Which five goods are the most expensive on Coll compared with on the mainland? Arrange the goods in rank order with the most expensive first and the least expensive last.

21   *The Village High Street. The buildings are traditional in design, built from stone probably of local origin.*

The cost of goods on Coll

GOODS	MINIMUM COLL PRICE AS A PERCENTAGE OF MAINLAND PRICE
Spaghetti	+ 150
Sugar	+ 35.5
Milk	+ 28
Flour	+ 91
Minced beef	+ 79
Potatoes	+ 87.5
Carrots	− 27
Apples	+ 46
Oranges	+ 50
Baked beans	+ 37
Cheddar cheese	+ 14
Sausages	+ 22
Tampax	+ 27
Coffee	+ 37
Lager	+ 86
Butter	+ 49
Sliced loaf	+ 63
Average	+ 46

Why do you think flour, spaghetti and potatoes are so much more expensive on Coll than on the mainland?

Only one thing costs less on Coll than on the mainland. Can you think why this might be?

Can you think of any reasons besides the cost of transporting goods that might push up the Coll prices? Think about the number of people who use the shops.

Changes in shopping

Over the past ten years there has been a change in the pattern of shopping all over Britain. People today tend to shop less often for convenience goods and to buy in bulk. They often travel to shop at large supermarkets or hypermarkets on the edge of town. Many prefer to shop in the evenings.

More women work full-time.
More people are paid monthly.
Many households have a freezer.
Many households own a car.

Use these statements to help you write a paragraph explaining why the pattern of shopping has changed.

The pattern of shopping on Coll has changed, too, but only markedly since electricity has come to the island. Before then, people relied on solid fuel or Calor gas for lighting and cooking. (The Hotel and a few houses had private generators). But with electricity, the islanders could enjoy the benefits of most electrical appliances including freezers. This meant that bulk-buying from the mainland became far more attractive.

What sort of goods might Collachs have ordered in bulk before freezers were available on the island?

The Hotel Shop still sells Calor gas. Why do you think there is no mains gas supply?

Convenience or comparison?

When you shop for clothes or shoes, you probably look in several shops and compare the quality and prices available before you make a decision. What other "comparison goods" do you buy sometimes that you do not need as often as convenience goods?

Collachs occasionally see visiting salesmen with a small selection of clothes and household goods, but they generally have to go to the mainland if they want to shop around. Oban is a busy tourist resort, but does not have a great selection of shops for buying comparison goods. Islanders will have to travel further if they want a big selection of shops to choose from. A shopping visit to Glasgow requires at least three days away from Coll and can be very expensive, involving travel and accommodation costs.

Shopping by mail order has become very popular throughout Britain and is particularly

useful to the islanders. Does your family ever use mail order? What do you think are the advantages and disadvantages of this method of shopping, particularly for Collachs?

Think about living on Coll. What do you think you would miss if you couldn't visit a town regularly?

22 Sheep being moved. Notice the road. Why do you think few lorries visit the island?

6

Summer visitors

The summer of 1985 was a particularly wet and cold one. Unable to sunbathe on the island's beaches, visitors dressed in their winter woollies, waterproofs and wellington boots to brave the gales and explore the island. Many of them had been on Coll before, but others were amazed at how wet the island became. Tessa, a regular visitor, commented to her friends on their first visit, "It's all right for you. You don't have to come here again . . . we're addicted to this island and *have* to put up with it."

Tessa's feelings about Coll are shared by many others who "have" to visit the island at least once a year, almost as though their lives depended upon an annual "dose" of its atmosphere. Why? What do these people do and where do they stay?

Sometimes in the summer, particularly on boat days, there seem to be so many people about in Arinagour that one wonders where they can all be staying! Some might only be visiting for a couple of hours, while the boat goes to Tiree. Look at the timetable on pages

23   The number of visitors to Coll during one year. There is no record of the exact number of visitors to Coll. This graph shows the general pattern.

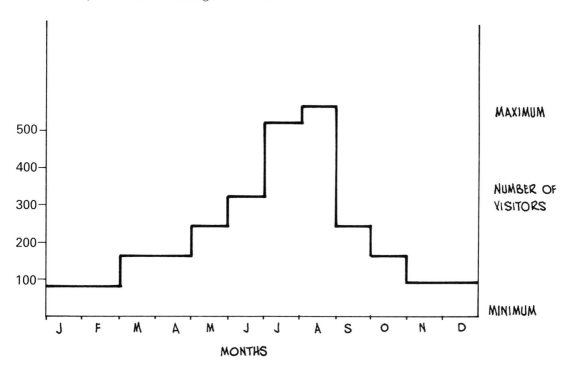

6-7. How long would day visitors have on Coll on a Wednesday in July?

Some visitors might have arrived by yacht and just be calling at the island for supplies and some time on dry land.

Many are there to stay for several days or weeks.

There are no figures available to show the exact numbers of visitors to Coll, but the graph (fig. 23) shows the pattern of visitor numbers throughout a year. Which months appear to have the most visitors? Which have the fewest? Can you think of any reasons for this pattern? What would you say is the "holiday season"?

In Chapter One, fig. 9, you discovered a large number of holiday homes. There are also a few houses and caravans which are owned by Collachs and let for self-catering holidays. Full board is available at the island's hotel and at the guest house. There are no camp sites, but some hardy visitors get permission from farmers to camp on their land. Many Collachs have friends and relations to stay for holidays.

Tourism as an industry

Only a few people on Coll depend totally on tourism for their livelihood (see the table), but those who do must make the most of the few months' holiday season.

Kevin and Julie Oliphant run the Coll Hotel, and as well as welcoming guests to stay, they are pleased to see day trippers or people staying in self-catering accommodation. Wherever they are staying, visitors often use some of the services provided by the hotel.

24   The Coll Hotel is now nearly twice the size of the original building. A modern extension has been added on the right-hand side. The whole hotel is painted white.

Employment created by tourism	
TYPE OF WORK	NUMBER OF JOBS CREATED
Hotel	6 full-time
Guest house	3 full-time
Café	1 full-time
Craft shop	1 part-time
Guided tours	1 part-time
Fishing and boat trips	Numerous part-time

Tourism also helps to keep the shops open and supplies a lot of passengers on the ferries.

These include:

Hire of bicycles
Guided tours of Coll
Bar, open 11 a.m. – 1 a.m.
Bar meals
Restaurant meals
Baths and showers
Sauna
Laundry service
Off licence

Which of these services do you think you would appreciate the most if you were renting a house for a holiday on Coll?

The Licensing Laws are different in Scotland from those in England. How much longer is the Coll bar open at a weekend than an English bar?

What sort of problems do you think a short season (the majority of the visitors arriving in only a few months of the year) creates for the Oliphants in keeping the hotel open all through the year?

Wildlife on Coll

For many of Coll's visitors the wildlife is a major attraction. The island's isolation has meant that wildlife has been virtually undisturbed. Seals can be seen all around the island shores and, in the summer months, hundreds of them bask in the sunshine on the rocks.

Otters, in danger of extinction in many parts of Britain, are often seen playing along the coast of Coll. They are more timid than seals, and visitors have to be quiet if they want to watch the animals for any length of time.

25   Seals basking in the sunshine.

26 A small whale beached at Crossapol.

On a summer's day, basking sharks might be seen close to the shore. These are harmless to humans and are fascinating to approach in a boat. The older sharks often have many barnacles stuck to them. Whales also visit Coll occasionally. Most of these are harmless to man, but people in boats have to be careful not to get too close to the dangerous killer-whale.

The sea birds on Coll are a great attraction to ornithologists. Oyster-catchers and other waders are commonly seen throughout the year, on the beaches, on the rocks and in the shallow waters near to the coast.

27 Oyster-catchers.

The lucky bird watcher might see the magnificent Peregrine falcons soaring around some of the island's cliff faces. Sea eagles from Mull pay occasional day visits to the island. There are many other birds, common and rare, that the ornithologist on Coll might be delighted to see.

In the summer, Coll is covered by a carpet of wild flowers and it is not uncommon to see a keen botanist on all fours looking for unusual species. Some very rare species of orchid are found on the island. Nobody wants to say exactly where they grow, for fear of their being destroyed.

How do you think the orchids might be threatened by too much publicity?

28 *Orchids thrive on Coll but are threatened with extinction elsewhere in Britain.*

29 Doing nothing on Coll. There are many colours in the layers of rock. ▼

▼ 30 Rockpools can be fascinating to look a

▼ 31 Sorisdale. A croft, popular with the visitors.

The attraction of Coll

Those who have never been to Coll often find it difficult to understand what it is that attracts people to the island. Below are some comments from visitors sharing their feelings about Coll.

"I just enjoy being able to do nothing. Life at home is so busy. There are no pressures on Coll."

"I love the people – locals and visitors. We always have a great social life on the island."

"I just unwind and relax."

"I love watching the birds. There are some very unusual sea birds on Coll shores."

"I enjoy having a wee dram and a chat with friends at the bar."

"The seals are my greatest love. I spend hours watching them. Occasionally I see otters. That's a great thrill."

"I enjoy fishing in the lochs and in the sea."

"The orchids are magnificent. So are the many other wild flowers."

"Peace."

What do these comments tell you about the types of holiday people have on Coll? Is there anything you would particularly like or dislike? Would you prefer to stay in a holiday camp or on Coll?

Plan a week's holiday on the island for either a family with two teenage children, or a middle-aged couple.

7

Harvesting the sea and the land

The waters around Coll are a valuable resource and provide much that can be used by the islanders.

Fish and shellfish

Some fish are caught locally and are used to bait creels or are kept for human consumption. They are not exported like the shellfish.

Lobsters are a delicacy served in many high-class European restaurants. These valuable shellfish provide some income for several islanders, who use small boats to fish for lobsters.

A lobster creel has to be baited, often with locally caught mackerel or other fish. A heavy weight makes sure that the creel lies on the sea bed, in shallow waters a few metres from the coast-line. The creel is attached by rope to a

32   John Brackenbury with lobsters.

33   A lobster fisherman's boat.

marker float. Sometimes several creels are joined on to one float. This is known as a "fleet".

Fishermen catch the float and haul up the creels. Any lobsters are removed, and their claws are tied so that they cannot pinch anyone or each other. The creels are re-baited and returned to the sea bed. The fishermen like to "lift" the creels once every day or two, but sometimes the sea is too rough for small boats to go out.

The lobsters are stored in "safes", wooden boxes anchored to the sea bed, a few metres below the low-tide mark. When they have a good stock and the prices are favourable, the fishermen send the lobsters to dealers in Oban. Many are then exported. During the autumn of 1985, John Brackenbury had several hundred lobsters in his safe. A severe storm destroyed it and many of his creels. In one night he lost

35 Crabs are commonly caught with the lobsters.

34 Lobster creel.

the income from several months' work.

Often, crabs are caught inside the lobster creels, too. There is a growing demand for certain types of crab, and some lobster fishermen are now selling these as well to dealers in Oban.

Whelks and mussels are found on Coll's shores and are often collected for local use or for selling.

Seaweed has a value

Seaweed has long been recognized as a useful fertilizer and there is plenty washed up on Coll's beaches. Farmers seldom use it, however, because they find it cheaper to buy fertilizer from the mainland than to spend long periods of valuable time collecting the seaweed.

Few trees

There are very few trees on Coll today, although there is evidence (roots, tree stumps and pollen) that, in the past, trees grew very

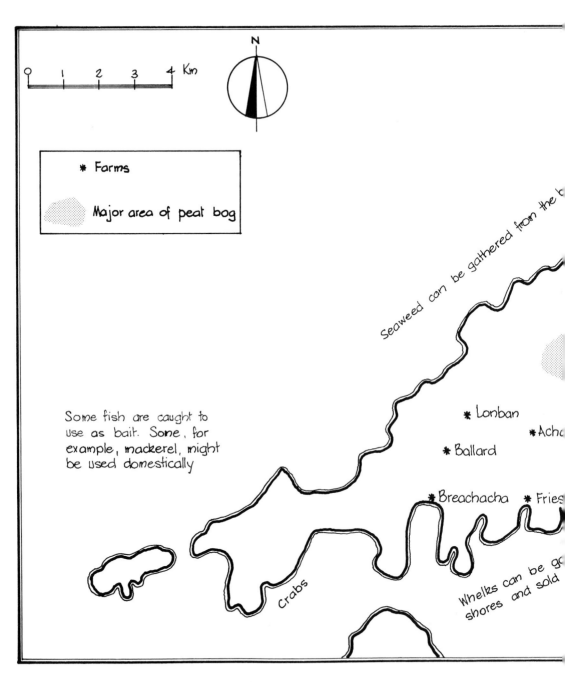

Major area of peat bog

Farms

* Farms

Some fish are caught to
use as bait. Some, for
example, mackerel, might
be used domestically

Seaweed can be gathered from the b

*Lonban

*Acha

*Ballard

*Breachacha *Fries

Crabs

Whelks can be g
shores and sold

well. About 9000 years ago, around 7000 B.C., there were large areas of forest on Coll. Scots pine, birch and some oak trees grew happily on the island. What happened?

As the ice from the last Ice Age melted, many areas were flooded. The soils of Coll's forests became waterlogged and, as the trees died, they were not replaced. The rotting vegetation eventually formed peat. Today there are several peat bogs on Coll. The main area is shown on the map, fig. 36. If the peat was covered in further deposits and

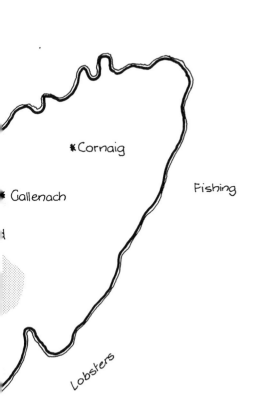

*Cornaig

* Gallenach

Fishing

Lobsters

undisturbed for some millions of years, it might turn to coal.

The waterlogged peat cannot support a forest, but, with the use of forestry ploughs to aerate and drain the soil, it would be possible to grow some trees, such as Sitka spruce and Lodgepole pine. In many parts of mainland Scotland, peat bogs have been drained and large areas of commercial forest have been established. David Ogg, a forester visiting Coll, commented that "A reasonable forest could be established on the island's peat bogs, but its very slow growth and the cost of transport are prohibitive. We wouldn't touch it."

The peat bogs of Coll do, however, have their uses. Every year, pieces of the soggy substance are cut from the peat banks. The peats are then stacked to dry out, before being carried out of the bog to island homes. The islanders burn pieces of peat on their fires.

Some coal is imported to the island, but peat remains a very important fuel.

37   Gordon cutting peats. Cutting peat and carrying it home is difficult work. Why do you think many islanders still choose to burn it in their fires?

38 The coal boat.

Farming

Poor soil coupled with haphazard weather conditions can make the Coll farmer's life very difficult. Careful choice of crops and animals, to survive the harsh environment, is very important if the farmer is to make a reasonable living.

The main farms on Coll are;

ACHA BREACHACHA }	Kenneth Stewart
BALLARD	Allan Brodie
CLIAD LONBAN }	Jock Galbraith and John Galbraith
GALLENACH	Mr De Vries
CORNAIG	Hamish Macrae
FRIESLAND	Indy and Colin Kennedy

Find these farms on the map, fig. 36.

Farming can be described as either "extensive" or "intensive". Arable farming, or the growing of crops, is more "intensive" than, for example, sheep farming. A lot of work has to go into one field of grain, but this produces a greater amount of food, or a higher yield, than the same area used for rearing sheep. Can you explain why market gardening (growing vegetables and flowers) is more intensive than sheep farming?

All the farming on Coll is "extensive", which means that the farms have to be quite large as each field produces a relatively small yield. Few crops are grown and these are virtually all used for feeding animals, except for potatoes, which are grown for human consumption. Coll farmers rely on the sale of their animals to make a living. Beef cattle and sheep are both important on Coll and in this chapter we will try to understand why this is.

In the late nineteenth and early twentieth centuries, cheese made on Coll was famous in many places, including the House of Commons. In 1940 there were 278 dairy cows on Coll, providing cream for the cheese which was made at Breachacha farm. However, the cheese industry died, as it could not compete against cheeses being made more cheaply elsewhere. Today there is no cheese being made on Coll.

Cattle

Some Coll farmers keep dairy cows to provide milk for domestic use. A cow only produces milk after she has had a calf. The farmer has to make sure that his cows have their calves at different times of the year so that he has a constant milk supply. The calves are kept with their mothers for a few weeks and then near to them for a few months, during which time they are fed on their mother's milk from a bucket. The farmer milks the cows twice a day, often by hand.

Friesians are common as Coll dairy cows. They are good because they produce high yields of milk – about 3 gallons a day. The same cows on an intensive dairy farm on the

Comparing the Coll Friesian with an intensive dairy farm Friesian

	COLL FRIESIAN	INTENSIVE DAIRY FARM FRIESIAN
PURPOSE	Domestic use by family. Excess milk fed to dogs and pigs (if any) or thrown away.	Commercial sales of milk to Milk Marketing Board. Milk used as milk and for making dairy products.
FEED	Grass and some additional feed, particularly in winter.	Intensive force-feeding for maximum yields.
CALVES	Kept on farm and fed from mother.	Sold within one week to another farmer, to be fostered by another cow or to be used for veal.

mainland might produce 6 or more gallons a day. Look at the table and see if you can write a few sentences explaining the differences in yields.

Rearing beef cattle is generally a less intensive type of farming than keeping dairy cattle. There are several different breeds of beef cattle on Coll, including Herefords, Highland, Short Horn and Aberdeen Angus. These are good on Coll as they are very hardy

39 Highland cows enjoying some of the good grazing on Breachacha farm. Notice how low and flat the land is, with no trees.

and can live outside through most or all of the winter. The only problem is periods of continuous rain in the winter which means that the cattle are constantly cold. Then they sometimes have to be taken in to byres for shelter as this is difficult to find outside.

Several farmers have bought Simmental bulls to run with the cows. These produce a heavier calf and thus more meat.

Bulls are kept with the cows in the fields all through the year and mating takes place as each cow comes into season, generally in the summer. Calves are born in the winter months, January – May. This is useful to the farmer, as this is the period of regular feeding (twice a day) and he can keep his eye on the cattle and give help to any cow that is in trouble giving birth. Sometimes a cow will be brought into the byre so that the farmer can watch her closely.

Most of the farmers' stock are reared on the island. Calves (and some older cows) are sold each year from October to December when they are about ten months old. Dealers at the markets in Oban and Stirling buy them to fatten up for meat. Farmers can get £200-£350 for a Hereford calf, depending on its quality and the market demand.

Why do you think the cattle are fattened elsewhere?

Sheep farming is an extensive type of farming, and sheep are to be seen everywhere on Coll – on the roadsides, in the fields, on rough grazing, even on the seashore. They are such an important part of the island scene that they deserve a whole chapter to themselves.

8

Sheep, sheep... and more sheep

If you spend your summer holidays on Coll, you can be sure you're sharing the island with around nine thousand sheep, including lambs. The sheep glossary gives you the meaning of some words used in sheep farming. They will help you to understand the following extracts from *The Sheep Farmer's Year*, by Allan Brodie, a Coll farmer.

40 *A young black-faced lamb is fascinated by the camera! The number on its side identifies the lamb to the farmers.*

Sheep glossary	
Ewe	female sheep
Hog	1-year-old sheep
Gimmer	2-year-old female sheep
Yeld ewe	barren ewe
Milk ewe	ewe rearing lambs
Tup	ram or male sheep
Clipping	shearing
Castrated	testicles removed, so infertile
Lambing	a time when sheep are giving birth to lambs

"The predominant breed, chosen mainly because of its hardiness and ability to survive on low quality grazing is the Blackface. The Blackface is also crossed with other breeds including the Cheviot and Border Leicester to produce a ewe capable of finding grass to eat on many parts of the island. Sheep on Coll, as elsewhere in Britain, suffer from a wide range of diseases, internal and external parasites and in some places mineral deficiencies."

There are no vets on Coll. Why is it important that the Coll farmers watch the condition of their animals very closely?

"Coll weather is also an important factor affecting the farmer's business. A cold wet winter can mean that the ewes are in poor condition at lambing time which leads to a high mortality rate in the lambs. High winds can mean that the ferry to Oban is unable to call at the pier when lambs are going to market and this further disrupts the farmer's plans.

"The sheep farmer's year begins around October/November when the ewes and gimmers are mated with the tups. It's important that the sheep are in good condition then to ensure a high proportion of twin lambs. A lean ewe is more likely to produce a single lamb or may not mate with the tup at all. Many Coll sheep are given supplementary feeding in the weeks prior to lambing to ensure that they are in reasonable condition and have a good supply of milk for their newborns.

"Lambing starts around mid-March and continues into May. This is the busiest time of the year for the sheep farmers when they can be observed trudging around the fields and hills with crook in hand and dog at heel. Depending on how the lambing is going it may or may not be safe to approach them! Their problems include ewes which need assistance at lambing, ewes with no milk but with twin lambs, ewes with plenty of milk but dead lambs, ewes which won't accept their own lambs but try to adopt other lambs."

The farmers might need to take home "pet" or orphan lambs. These will have to be kept warm and regularly bottle-fed with milk. How do you think your household would adapt to looking after a "pet" lamb?

"A short time after lambing has finished the lambs' tails are 'docked', i.e. about half is cut off, the owner's earmark is put on the lambs and the tup lambs are castrated. The lambs are also counted and the 'lambing percentage' calculated by comparing the

41 *Sheep on the pier awaiting their turn to be loaded on to the boat.*

42 *Two young visitors to the island enjoy looking after a "pet" lamb.*

number of lambs with the number of ewes and gimmers put to the tup. This whole operation is known as 'the marking'. Percentages of 100% and over are quite common on Coll which is generally recognised to be good for this part of Scotland.

"Clipping of all sheep takes place during June and July, the hogs and yeld ewes in June and the milk ewes in July. Much of the clipping on Coll is now done by a gang of clippers made up of islanders and mainlanders using electric shearing

43 *Twin lambs are common on Coll.*

machines, though some farmers still shear their own. Dry weather and a good 'rise' are essential to the clipping. 'Rise' means the soft new wool close to the sheep's skin and grown that year and a sheep with little or no 'rise' is very difficult to clip. The wool is packed into large sacks and sent to wool merchants on the mainland where every fleece is graded and priced accordingly.

"Marketing of lambs takes place from August onwards, many being sold for immediate slaughter, the remainder to mainland farmers for further fattening. Ewe lambs suitable for breeding are kept and put to the tup two years later as gimmers. Once all the lambs have been 'spained' (i.e. separated) from the ewes the whole cycle starts again in October and November with the ewes and tups being joined once more."

Asked what particular problems faced farmers on Coll, Kenneth Stewart replied:

"The weather is the main thing. Of course, all British farmers are affected by the weather, but it can affect our transport . . . it can be a real problem if the boat doesn't get in when you've got 300 lambs waiting on the pier to go to the market. You have to walk them to the village from the farm and so when the boat misses you have to walk them home again and try again for the next market. . . . You pick the market that you think will give the best price for your particular stock, so it's important to be there."

How far does Kenneth Stewart have to walk his lambs from Breachacha to the pier? How long would this take?

A ticket to Oban

Each sheep or cow needs a ticket on the boat. If the farmer's bill for one journey comes to over £100, he gets a single ticket free. He will have to pay for his return journey and for anybody who goes to help him. In Oban he will have to pay for accommodation for two nights.

The Farmer's Year

JAN	Plough fields for crops so that the frost can kill any roots.
FEB	Plough dung and seaweed into fields.
MAR	Rotovate*, harrow and disc* fields ready for sowing.
APR	Sow kale, oats, silage and potatoes. Lambing begins. Visit sheep at least twice a day.
MAY	Sow turnips. Lambing continues.
JUN	Sow rape. Shear hogs and tups.
JUL	Harvest hay and make silage. Clip ewes.
AUG	Harvest hay and make silage.
SEP	Ditto if weather has been bad.
OCT	Maintenance.
NOV	Tups to ewes.
DEC	Feeding cattle and some sheep.

JAN–MAR: Feed cattle twice daily in fields (DEC–MAY) and some sheep, e.g. tups.

AUG–DEC: Maintenance of farm and machinery. For example, drainage, fencing, servicing of machines.

* Rotovating and discing are two ways in which the farmer prepares the soil for sowing (or planting) with seed. The machines cut up the clods of soil to make it fine. Rotovating cuts deeper into the soil than discing.

This could result in a bill of about £100. With these expenses the farmer needs to be sure of getting the best price for his animals if he is to make a profit.

The table summarises the Coll farmer's year. Use this to help you write a few paragraphs about his working life. Remember to include things that make Coll farming different from farming on the mainland. Remember to think about arable and cattle farming as well as about sheep. Use the seasons, Spring, Summer, Autumn and Winter, as headings to help you.

9

Industrial Coll

Any business needs to make a profit to be successful. This means that the price of the finished product must be greater than all the expenses involved in making it. For example, if it costs £1.50 to make an item that sells for £2.00, then the profit is 50p.

Convenience goods in particular must sell at a reasonable price if they are to be competitive. Luxury goods are "comparison" goods (see page 25) and do not have to rely so much on selling at the lowest price. Can you suggest why?

44 The Highlands and Islands region.

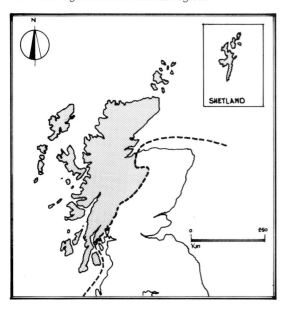

The H.I.D.B.

Coll is in the area of the Highlands and Islands of Scotland. This is an administrative area looked after by the Highlands and Islands Development Board (H.I.D.B.). The H.I.D.B. is financed by the government, which means that all British taxpayers contribute towards its work. Many governments have been worried by the depopulation of isolated areas of Scotland. To encourage people to stay in these areas, the H.I.D.B. has two major aims:

1. To help the people of the Highlands and Islands by providing job opportunities and improving social conditions.
2. To enable the Highlands and Islands to contribute more to Britain's wealth.

Creating better job opportunities means that more people can earn and spend money and so help to make the area richer. People will also then be able to improve their own social conditions.

Tourism can create jobs and help to keep people in an area, and the H.I.D.B. is pleased to encourage this service industry. On Coll it has also provided grants to farmers and to fishermen and to help maintain facilities used by the community, such as the village hall.

The cost of keeping the Coll village hall is much higher than any income the hall can make through being let out for occasions such as dances. Why do you think the H.I.D.B. considers it important to keep the hall for the community?

The H.I.D.B. is keen to develop small

45 *Hebridean Herbals.*

industries in the area. It can offer advice and financial help in the form of loans or grants.

Keen to see some manufacturing industry on Coll, the H.I.D.B. renovated an old school to make a modern factory for Hebridean Herbals. In 1974, Wendy McKechnie started "Coll Herbals", producing luxury skin-care products from her home on the island. The business has grown and now, under its new name, Hebridean Herbals, employs about five and sometimes, during busy times, as many as ten people.

The cost of freight for raw materials such as lanolin, and for the finished product, is certainly high. Why do you think Hebridean Herbals can survive freight costs, when a cake factory on Coll could not?

When Wendy wants to talk to her suppliers or customers on the mainland, she must either make a long-distance telephone call or make a visit involving at least one night away from home. Why do you think it is important that Wendy visits her suppliers and her customers occasionally?

Project Trust

47 *Volunteers at Bousd.*

"Ringing telephones, clicking computers, tapping telex and typewriters." This might describe a high-tec office anywhere in the country. In fact, this is the Head Office of Project Trust at Bousd on the Isle of Coll.

Project Trust was set up in 1976, with the aim of helping school leavers in Britain to gain some understanding of life outside Europe, and particularly in the Third World.

Volunteers for the Project are interviewed in their home areas. If successful, they then attend a four-day selection course on Coll, where they have the opportunity to learn about some of the countries they might visit, as well as to display some of the skills that might be useful in those areas. Those who gain a place with Project Trust will work for a year in one of many places.

The countries where volunteers from Project Trust are sent to work are: Australia, Egypt, Hong Kong, Honduras, India, Indonesia, Jamaica, Jordan, Kenya, South Africa, Sri Lanka, Sudan. Look for these countries on an atlas map of the world. Are most of them north or south of the equator? How many are "tropical", that is, lie between the Tropic of Cancer in the north and the Tropic of Capricorn in the south? Do you think most of the countries could be described as "poor" or as "rich"?

46 *Project Trust logo.*

It is vitally important to the success of Project Trust that volunteers are placed in a job to which they are well-suited. There are a variety of opportunities available, including working in a school, on a farm, or in a hospital. The whole operation is organized from Coll. Any problems, such as a volunteer being ill and having to return home suddenly, are dealt with at the Head Office on Coll.

How can Project Trust operate from such an isolated position? Clue: High-Tec.

Project Trust has helped the island economically and socially, employing between four and six full-time workers at Bousd. In addition, five house-holders are paid to play host to the volunteers who come to the selection courses. There are normally fourteen volunteers staying for four nights, about fourteen times a year.

Why Coll?

Coll is an ideal location for Project Trust's headquarters, but there are many other places that would have been suitable, so why was Coll chosen?

The Director of Project Trust, Major Nicholas MacLean-Bristol, has family connections with Coll, going back for hundreds of years. He first visited the island in the 1950s and decided that

BALLYHOUGH

48 Architect's view of Ballyhough. The original building is in the middle of the complex. Look through the book at all the pictures which show buildings. Which design do you like the best?

he would like to live on Coll and bring his family back to the island.

In 1962, Prince Alexander Desta of Ethiopia asked his friend Major MacLean if he would leave the Army and help him run Ethiopia. The Major replied that his future was in the Hebrides but that he would send "first-rate people from the U.K." and that "it was up to him [the Prince] to make them fall in love with Ethiopia".

The location of Project Trust's headquarters, then, is not an accident. Coll was not chosen only because of its suitability, but rather because of Major MacLean's links with the island. Many modern industries are similarly where they are as a result of personal reasons. For example, the director of a computer software company may choose to be in an area where there are good leisure facilities. Industries like this, which do not rely on being near to certain things such as raw materials or the market, are described as "footloose".

Can you think of any other types of industry that are "footloose"?

The H.I.D.B. recognizes the value of Project Trust to Coll and has sponsored the development of new headquarters at Ballyhough.

How do you think Project Trust improves the economy and social conditions of Coll?

Do you think it is important that the H.I.D.B. helps small communities like Coll? Can you explain your answer?

10

999 emergency

Over most of mainland Britain, the Police, Ambulance Service, Fire Brigade or Bomb Disposal Squad could be at your home within minutes of your dialling 999. In coastal areas you could also alert the Coastguard and the Lifeboat Service.

On Coll you can dial 999 and tell the G.P.O. switchboard in Oban which service you require, but from then on things are very different. There are no police on Coll. There is no hospital to send you an ambulance. There are no fire engines to rush to your home with their sirens blaring, or bomb disposal squads to clear the area if a suspicious-looking parcel is left unattended. There are no full-time coastguards and there is no lifeboat. In this chapter, we shall be discovering some of the ways in which the people of Coll deal with emergency situations.

With such a small community of people it is important that everyone gets on well together. Obviously, there are arguments and disagreements, but generally these are forgotten quickly. The Collachs trust each other so well that they often leave cars unlocked and with the keys in the ignition.

Why are people in Britain generally more particular about locking up cars and possessions?

Police

Fortunately, there is little call for police in Coll, though in recent years there have been some petty thefts from private homes. Police from Tiree have come to Coll to investigate these, but they have not always been able to catch the culprits. Anti-social behaviour like this threatens to destroy the trust between the people of Coll – one of the things that makes the island such a special place.

Routine visits are made to the island by the police from Tiree or from Oban. They might come to check things such as shot-gun licences or extended bar licences for events such as a dance; to ensure that farmers are keeping to the laws regarding the dipping of sheep; and to check that cars are road-worthy – though, since there is no garage on the island, cars do not need to have an M.O.T. certificate.

If there was a real emergency on Coll and the police were required urgently, a helicopter would be chartered to bring them over from Oban or Glasgow.

Can you think of any advantages and disadvantages to the community of there being no permanent policeman on Coll?

Fire

If a Collach dials 999 and asks for the fire service, the G.P.O. will try to contact Ian Burnside (his name's actually Kennedy, but he used to live at Burnside). Ian works during the day on the island's roads, making sure they are safe, and it might be some time before he can be found. The "Coll Fire Brigade" consists of many of the island's men who must all be gathered together from across the island. There is no fire engine, but in Arinagour there is a fire shed, which houses a trailer containing water pumps, hoses, ladders, protective clothing and torches. This trailer is connected to any available vehicle and driven as near as possible to the fire.

Which houses on the island do you think would stand the least chance of being saved from fire? Why? Look at a map of your local area and find out how far it is from the local fire station to your home. How quickly do you think the Fire Brigade could reach you in an emergency?

Four times a year the "Coll Fire Brigade" has a training session led by firemen from the mainland. Speed is essential if fires are to be put out before there is too much damage.

Ambulance

Two Coll farmers sit in the small waiting room at the doctor's surgery in Arinagour. They are discussing the state of the silage crop and the effects of the heavy rain on this year's hay. Music from a tape recorder prevents conversation in the surgery being heard in the waiting room, through the thin partition wall.

Patients may have to wait a little longer than you do in your local surgery, as the doctor has to run the surgery single-handed, and prepare the medicines, because there is no chemist on the island. There is one district nurse on Coll who visits patients requiring regular treatment in their homes.

Think about your own doctor's surgery. Perhaps you go to a health centre. How many people besides the doctor work there? Which jobs will the Coll doctor have to do that your doctor would not normally have to do?

Dr De Mornay believes very strongly that the islanders deserve the same high standard of medical care as those living on the British mainland. There are some tests that can be done in the surgery, but very often blood and urine samples must be sent to the nearest hospital in Oban for analysis. These specimens must be as fresh as possible and so the doctor will take them shortly before the boat leaves Coll. If bad weather prevents the boat's arrival at Coll the tests may have to be delayed.

How long might a patient have to wait in the winter before fresh specimens can be sent? Look at the timetable of ship sailings on pages 6-7 to help you.

When someone is very sick and requires hospital care, an air ambulance must be called to collect the patient. The doctor will telephone Loganair, an air company in Glasgow, and arrange a time for a plane to land, weather permitting.

Emergency medical cases can occur at any time. If an air ambulance is expected, Allan Brodie might have to leave his farm work to clear the cattle and sheep off his field at Ballard. It is a fairly flat, long field, with painted railings at either end, and acts as the island's only airstrip. John James must be called to ensure that the wind sock is blowing and the field is as safe as possible for the plane's arrival. He might also have to help load the patient on to the small plane.

Why do you think it is so important that the wind sock is blowing when a plane is expected?

Small aeroplanes called "Islanders" are used. They are most suitable because they can take off and land over a short distance on rough surfaces.

There are no lights on the airstrip and, at night, an Air-Sea Rescue Helicopter must come if there is an emergency. Car headlights might be used to show the landing site. These big helicopters are sometimes used for daytime emergencies if the weather is too rough for the aeroplane. In severe weather conditions it might be several hours or even days before an air ambulance can reach the island.

Aeroplanes are a rare sight on Coll and news spreads quickly if the ambulance plane is seen. It is not long before most people on the island know who has been flown away to hospital in Glasgow.

Look at the map of Scotland, fig. 2. How far does the ambulance have to fly from Coll to Glasgow? How far is it from your home to the nearest hospital?

Very rarely are patients flown home to Coll

49 Air ambulance on Coll. Pilots do not like landing when there have been a lot of cows grazing on the airstrip, as the "plane gets so dirty".

when they are discharged from hospital. They usually have to travel from Glasgow to Oban and catch the ferry back to the island.

Think about the problems a Coll family would face if they had a teenage son or daughter in hospital in Glasgow for a month. How do they compare with the difficulties a family on the mainland might have?

Coastguard

The seas around the Hebrides can be extremely treacherous and an efficient coastguard service is essential. We shall discover some of the ways in which lives can be saved in Chapter 11 – "Gale warning".

11

Gale warning

For many people living along the coastline of Britain, the shipping forecast, given regularly on Radio 4, is essential listening.

Look at fig. 50. Which sea area is Coll in? Which is the sea area nearest to your home? Try to listen to a shipping forecast and compare the reports for the two areas.

Immediately after the forecasts for each shipping area is a report from meteorological stations. The first is from Tiree, Coll's neighbouring island. Sometimes you will see Tiree mentioned in the "top ten" for daily weather, as the island is well-known for having the longest spells of sunshine on the west coast of Britain.

Wind speed is measured by the Beaufort Scale. Look at fig. 51. If a flag were blowing outside your window at this moment, what do you think it would look like? Can you estimate the scale for the wind that is blowing? What effect do you think a severe storm force 11 would have on your home?

> "Attention all shipping. There is a warning of a gale in sea areas Rockall, Malin and Hebrides. Storm force 10, increasing to severe storm force 11 imminent."

Occasionally, radio programmes might be interrupted with a gale warning like this. Such an announcement might send fishermen down to the shore to pull their boats further up the beach and to make doubly sure that they are securely tied. Collachs thinking of going fishing will stay at home. Gales can blow for several days and islanders trying to get home from the mainland might spend a long time on the boat,

sometimes seeing the island, knowing that they are close to home, but also knowing that conditions are too bad for the boat to get to the pier.

Cold winds can blow rain horizontally and make life very uncomfortable, particularly for farmers. Some animals have to be fed every day in the winter, whatever the weather. Dairy cattle must be milked in the morning and evening.

Any boat at sea during a gale is at great risk, although of course the sea is dangerous at any time. The Coastguard service has saved many lives along Britain's coast.

Coastguard

John James is the Chief Coastguard on Coll. He could be fishing for lobsters, watching the television, sound asleep in bed or enjoying a drink at the hotel when "Bleep bleep" from his bleeper will send him rushing to the telephone. Oban Coastguard Station tells him that a yacht with a family of six aboard is in trouble by the Cairns, off the north-east coast of Coll. Very quickly, John might find some of the volunteer Coastguards at the hotel and he can quickly allocate jobs to them. Margaret, John's wife, will telephone all the men living outside the village. John English and Iain Cochrain might go and collect all the equipment from the Coastguard store, while John James sends two distress maroons (bright flares) 400 metres into the air to alert any men living in Arinagour.

About twenty men will make their way as

55° 50° 45° 40° 35° 30° 25° 20° 15° 10° 5°W 0° 5°E 10° 15°

NORTH
ICELAND

DENMARK
STRAIT

NORTH
UTSIRE

SOUTH
UTSIRE

SOUTH-EAST
ICELAND

VIKING

FAEROES

FAIR ISLE

FISHER

WEST
NORTHERN
SECTION

EAST
NORTHERN
SECTION

BAILEY

HEBRIDES BL

CROM-
ARTY

FORTIES

GERMAN
BIGHT

FORTH

DOGGER

B

TYNE

HUMBER

T

D

ROCKALL

MALIN

M

R
IRISH
SEA

THAMES

RS DOVER

WIGHT

LUNDY

PORT
LAND

Va

FASTNET

C

WEST
CENTRAL
SECTION

EAST
CENTRAL
SECTION

SHANNON

S

PLYMOUTH

SOLE

BISCAY

FINISTERRE

WEST
SOUTHERN
SECTION

EAST
SOUTHERN
SECTION

TRAFALGAR

35° 30° 25° 20° 15°

STATIONS WHOS
REPORTS ARE BROA
THE 5 MINUTE FO
T   Tiree
BL   Butt of Lewis
Su   Sumburgh
B   Bell Rock
D   Dowsing
V   Dover or Var
RS   Royal Sovere
C   Channel Ligh
S   Scilly
Va   Valentia
R   Ronaldsway
M   Malin Head
J   Jersey

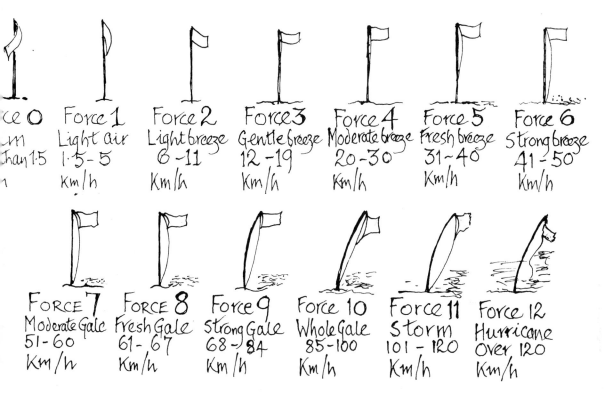

ce 0   Force 1   Force 2   Force 3   Force 4   Force 5   Force 6
m   Light air Light breeze Gentle breeze Moderate breeze Fresh breeze Strong breeze
than 1·5 1·5-5   6-11   12-19   20-30   31-40   41-50
       Km/h   Km/h   Km/h   Km/h   Km/h   Km/h

FORCE 7   FORCE 8   Force 9   Force 10   Force 11   Force 12
Moderate Gale Fresh Gale Strong Gale Whole Gale Storm   Hurricane
51-60   61-67   68-84   85-100   101-120   Over 120
Km/h   Km/h   Km/h   Km/h   Km/h   Km/h

50   Sea areas. (From Meteorological Office Leaflet No. 3).

51   The Beaufort Scale. The strength of the wind is indicated by the number.

quickly as they can, by car or by tractor, to Sorisdale. There they will have to walk over hills and bog for about two kilometres to the stretch of coast nearest to the yacht.

The lifeboat will be on its way from Mallaig or from Islay, depending on which way the wind is blowing. Look at fig. 2. Which boat do you think is most likely to be called if the wind is blowing from the south?

The men of the Coastguard offer to take the family ashore. If the lifeboat hasn't arrived, this may involve using the "Breeches buoy", a life-saving method that has won the Coll Coastguard a National Award for their speed and efficiency.

A helicopter might have been called to the scene, particularly if the boat is in great danger. How do you think a helicopter will be able to help with the rescue? The doctor might be on

the shore as well, and, if any survivors need hospital treatment, they might be taken straight to Oban in the lifeboat or by helicopter.

The Coll Coastguard are usually called out about eight times a year. Of the seven jobs that John James has, he finds the Coastguard the most demanding and often the most rewarding. There may be two or three times when the men are called out during a bitterly cold, wet winter's night, on a false alarm. These occasions are very frustrating for everyone concerned, but as John James says, "They are well made up for by being able, on another day, to help save a life."

Imagine that someone in your household is a volunteer Coastguard. How do you think emergency calls in the middle of the night could affect your family?

12

Coll and the future

What about the future of Coll? The H.I.D.B., local council, national government, E.E.C. Parliament and other official bodies all want to encourage people to live and work on Coll, so that a community will remain on the island.

Proposals have been made to develop housing and to improve the roads. Tourism is to be encouraged. Kevin Oliphant, for one, is certainly keen that the island should prosper. "Coll's going to grow . . .," he said, and he is determined to do all that he can to prove this. However, the number of young people on the island is decreasing as they move to the mainland for work and for other attractions, not available on Coll.

How could you encourage young people back to live and work on Coll? Could industrial developments be profitable? Would they spoil the environment?

The cost of Coll

Some people think that helping Coll is a waste of the British taxpayers' money. They might prefer to see the island left to survive on its own with no outside support, even if this meant that there would be few, if any, inhabitants.

Coll is just one example of an isolated community. There are many others in Britain, in Europe and in the rest of the world. The Falkland Islands are a famous example. Some people consider that communities like Coll and the Falklands are far too expensive to support. Others think that they are an essential part of the British scene. Look at the following thoughts of a variety of people.

"I strongly object to my taxes being used to help keep such a small community going."

"I don't see why the islanders should have to pay so much extra for everything. They should be able to live on the same level as the rest of Britain, without extra expense."

"It is ridiculous paying for one teacher and one school with only five children."

"I wish more could be done to make life on Coll

52 *Will these children return to Coll when they leave school?*

attractive to school leavers. It is such a shame that they don't want to come back to the island."

"Coll has many unusual sites for wild flowers and animals (flora and fauna). I think that the island should be made into a nature reserve."

"It is so important that isolated communities should survive."

Imagine that you are a planner with the H.I.D.B. You are in charge of an area including Coll. The rest of the area has many centres of employment. Coll is the only place in your area that is proving to be particularly expensive to the H.I.D.B. Write a report for the *Oban Times* explaining why you think the H.I.D.B. should continue to support Coll as much as it can.

53   *Could Coll become an island of ruined crofts?*

Glossary

byre cow shed.

Caledonian Macbrayne ferry operators to Coll.

child-adult segregation children and adults kept apart.

comparison goods high-order goods that you do not need every day. You shop around for them, before you buy.

convenience goods goods that you require regularly, for example, bread and gloves. It is important that these are convenient to buy.

depopulation decrease in the number of people. For example, depopulation might be caused by people moving away.

descendants later generations of the family.

dram a drink of whisky.

emigrate move out of a country.

fertilizer substance to make soil more fertile, so that it will grow more.

freight goods being transported.

gale force strong winds of force 8 or more on the Beaufort Scale.

high tec(h) advanced, modern equipment, such as computers.

holiday season period of time that is important for holidays.

hypermarket very large store, usually on the edge of a town. Sells a wide range of goods.

mainland the main area of Britain, not including offshore islands.

master of ceremonies person who announces dances and organizes people at social events. Often just called M.C.

mortality rate number of deaths in one year per 1000 of population.

parasite an animal or plant that lives on another, often to the disadvantage of the host.

predominant strongest or the major type.

primary industry industry involved in working the earth's surface. Farming, fishing, forestry and mining.

secondary industry manufacturing and construction industries.

Simmental a continental breed of cattle.

study bedroom a room used as a study and also as a bedroom.

tertiary industry industries that provide a service, for example, shops, hotels, teaching.

waterlogged saturated with water. Can hold no more.

windsock a hollow tube hanging from a pole. Position of the windsock indicates the direction and strength of the wind.

Island Information

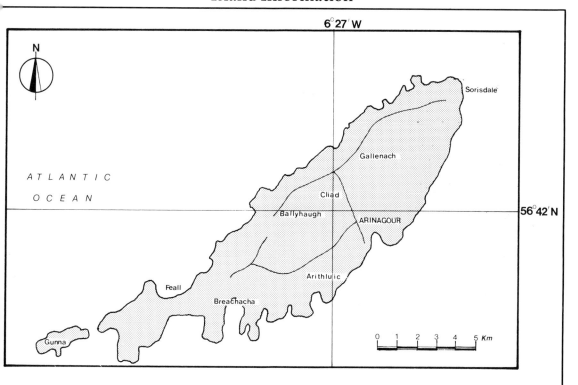

Area: Approximately 75 square kilometres or 7500 hectares.

Population: 140.

Population density: 1 – 2 people per square kilometre.

Language: English. About 25% of the population also speak Gaelic.

Transport: Ferry service from Oban. No public transport on the island.

Economy: Farming, fishing, herbal cosmetics, tourism.

Government: Nationally from Whitehall. Regionally from Strathclyde and from the Highlands and Islands Development Board in Inverness.

Wildlife commonly seen on and around Coll:
Rabbits, hares and hedgehogs.
More than a hundred different bird species.
Seals and otters.
Visiting basking sharks and whales.

Index